Introduction

Most test-taking guides start out with something like this:

(1)Get plenty of rest
(2)Eat a good breakfast

Yada, yada, yada…

With years of test-taking experience now under my belt, I have determined what is truly important and useful. In doing so, I have eliminated topics of dubious relevance, downplayed purely theoretical concepts, and minimized the use of extensive calculations and elaborate vocabulary to illustrate points that are either intuitively obvious or of limited practical use.

In other words, I have trimmed all the fat. As a result of this process, what you are now holding in your hands is my *Prescription for Test-Taking Success: The D.K.E.S. Formulation*.

I hope you enjoy digesting it as much as I enjoyed writing it.

The D.K.E.S. Formulation

- Desire
- Knowledge
- Endurance
- Speed

Learning should be desired
and welcomed
not forced.

The D.K.E.S. Formulation

Desire

Knowledge

Endurance

Speed

DESIRE

The 1st step to successful test-taking is to clearly state why you are taking the test you are preparing for in the first place. What are you trying to accomplish? What goal do you want to achieve?

If you cannot complete this next statement, then your test-taking deficiency is a lack of desire or goal setting:

"I am about to take this ______________________________, **and**

(*whatever test it is*)

score at least ______________________, **so that I can**

(*whatever goal score you have in mind*)

____."

(*whatever ultimate goal you're trying to achieve*)

Your goal does not have to be elaborately stated or grammatically correct, and you can have more than one. The point of this exercise is that you must state at least one… preferably, one that is the difference between life as you know it and life as you would like it to be. In other words, it should be a life-changing goal, something that you desperately want to accomplish and really, really need to accomplish.

Test-taking should be expected not feared.

The D.K.E.S. Formulation

- Desire
- Knowledge
- Endurance
- Speed

KNOWLEDGE

God has granted you free will. In other words, you have the power to make a choice. Knowledge itself is power. So, with even more of it, you are bound to make a better, more informed choice about whatever test question (*or issue*) you may be facing.

So, how much knowledge pertaining to the test content do you have? How much more do you need? How will you go about getting it?

If you are unable to complete this next statement with the recommended text below the blank line, your test-taking problem consists of a significant knowledge deficit:

"I know ____________________________________ about this test,

(*recommended text:* all there is to know)

because I learned all about it from resources produced by

___________________________________."

(*recommended text:* the creators of the test)

You cannot expect to score well on a test you know hardly anything about. Whether it is a subject area test or a standardized exam, you must become intimately familiar with the concept(s) that will be covered on the test. Period. And, the people who are best positioned to teach you about what's going to be on the test are the makers of the test. For example, these people could be the makers of the ACT®, or the person who teaches you English II. No matter who it is, they most likely have created a resource (*or a few of them*) to help you prepare for the exam. Do whatever you need to do to get your hands on that resource – *don't break any laws, of course.* Then, review that resource carefully, as though your life depends on it. Learn everything there is to know about the test.

Which brings me to another very important aspect of knowledge enhancement - discovering how you learn best. Do you learn best from reading the material or hearing the material? Do you prefer lectures or hands-on activities? Do you like the room where you're studying to be totally quiet, or do you prefer music to be playing in the background? Identify the most effective study technique for yourself and study that way.

It is next-to-impossible to attain knowledge without knowing how to read. Let me take that a step further: It is very difficult to attain knowledge without accurately comprehending what you read. You see, it's one thing to know how to read, and it's another thing entirely to understand or comprehend what you've read.

Thank God, knowledge can be supplemented and enhanced, and reading comprehension skills can be improved. Test-taking coaches and tutors can help you to determine what your strengths and weaknesses are in different areas, and they can also help to improve your reading comprehension. Teachers at school can also teach you about the test for which you are preparing and help you to create a customized study schedule that fits your unique needs and circumstances. You can also take advantage of the free 1-hour consultation that accompanies your purchase of this ebook, so that I can help you decide which route may be best for you to take.

Repetition teaches a dear school, and practice makes permanent.

The D.K.E.S. Formulation

- Desire
- Knowledge
- **Endurance**
- Speed

ENDURANCE

To score well on any test, you must have what I like to refer to as "stick-to-it-ness". Others call it *endurance*. Some call it *faith*. No matter what you choose to call it, this is what it means: It is what it is. Don't cry over spilled milk. So what if you failed a course or some standardized exam three times! First, forgive yourself – this is a crucial step. Then, recite this prayer:

"Dear Lord, I forgive myself for messing up, and I know you forgive me, too. You made me. You know that I'm human and that I will make mistakes. I know that with Your help I can do better, and apart from You I can do nothing. Help me to acknowledge that yesterday has passed and tomorrow is not promised. Empower me to live my best life for You in this present moment and to achieve the greatest impact for Your glory. Help me to get up, dust myself off, and go on in Your name. In Jesus' name I do humbly pray, Amen."

Then ~

Get up. Dust yourself off. Regroup by getting some expert advice on how to move forward with a different approach. In other words, don't be ashamed to ask for help. Try again. Don't give up. Finish what you started.

If you are not 110% dedicated to finishing some test and reaching your goal, you have a significant endurance deficiency.

To fix this problem, you must practice on the test content again and again and again. Then, practice some more!

So, hang in there and find as many practice test questions or writing prompts as you possibly can. You can even ask a teacher or other trusted person for suggestions of additional resources. You'll be surprised at what's available to help you.

Test-taking is like a sport. You must be mentally and physically prepared for it.

The D.K.E.S. Formulation

- Desire
- Knowledge
- Endurance
- **Speed**

SPEED

Like with any other sport, you must work at getting better at taking tests. Even more importantly, you should have fun doing it. Yes, I said that right: Have fun doing it!

Just think about it – taking a test gives you the opportunity to strut your stuff. It is a time for you to shine. So, why not have fun doing it?

If you have a strong desire to score well, have strengthened your knowledge base, and improved your endurance, this final step should be a piece of cake.

It only requires you to simulate a real-live test, complete with the pressure of time limits. And really, you don't have to take a complete exam. You can break the test up into components, set your alarm for the appropriate time limit plus about thirty seconds, which should be ample time to put the alarm down and get situated. When the buzzer goes off, STOP!

STOP!

STOP!

Sorry! I didn't mean to yell.

But seriously, stop taking the test and turn the alarm, (*which should still be screeching at this point*), off.

If you had a chance to review all the questions, carefully consider them, and respond to all of them, your speed is on-point. If you did not, then you have a significant speed deficit.

Check your answers against the answer key. Honestly grade your work and determine why you missed the ones you did, if you missed any at all!

I stress that in the case of inaccurate responses, you should not attempt to move on until you fully understand why the answer you chose is wrong.

Then, repeat this "Speed" step until you get faster with improved accuracy.

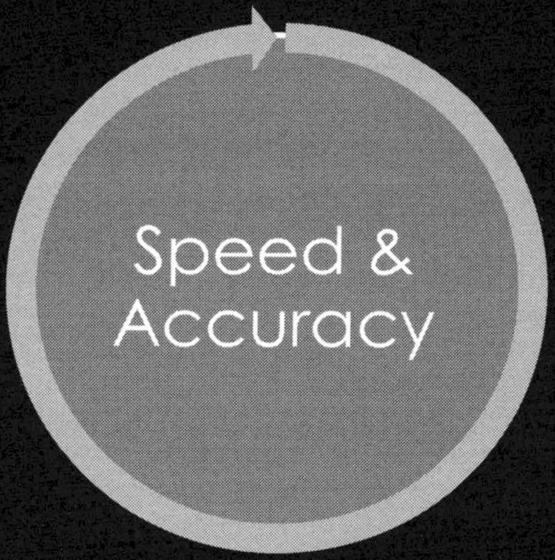

And keep repeating this step until the day of your test.

The D.K.E.S. Formulation

- Desire
- Knowledge
- Endurance
- Speed

1-Hour Consultation Offer

Although I am working full-time, finishing my MBA, and working on software that will help aspiring Mississippi barbers to prepare for the state licensure exam, I am dedicated to honoring the 1-hour phone or webinar consultation I promised with your purchase of this book. So, if you'd like to take advantage of spending some quality time with me either by phone or via the internet to discuss your test-taking deficit(s) and specific steps you can take to improve it/them, please drop me a note at kmliddellmd@aol.com.

Final Words from the Author

Thank you so much for reading this book. I hope you found at least one thing in it beneficial.

Remember: Be an active participant in your learning process, and you will definitely get out what you put in.

Made in the USA
Monee, IL
04 November 2026

67383431R00016